Getting Laid (Off)

A Multi-media Experiment in Laughing in the Face of Job Loss, a Crumbling Economy and Other Calamities. (No kidding!)

Rodney Curtis

Read The Spirit Books
an imprint of
David Crumm Media, LLC
Canton, Michigan

For more information and further discussion, visit
www.Getting-Laid-Off.com

Copyright © 2013 by Rodney Curtis
All Rights Reserved
ISBN: 978-1-939880-15-4
Version 1.0 2013-11-01

Cover art and design by
Rick Nease
www.RickNeaseArt.com

Published by
Read The Spirit Books
an imprint of
David Crumm Media, LLC
42015 Ford Rd., Suite 234
Canton, Michigan, USA

For information about customized editions, bulk purchases or permissions, contact David Crumm Media, LLC at info@DavidCrummMedia.com

Contents

Dedication	v
Disclaimer or Preface or Author running his mouth off	vi
Humor in Hard Times	1
Thoughts Running Through My Head as I'm Getting Laid Off	4
Not All Who Wander	6
Salivation Army	9
Blatant Attempt to Get on Marketplace	12
Cost Saving Tips	15
Until Now, I've Never Lied on My Resume	18
Goaded by My Goatee	20
Marvin and Me	23
Laid Back or Laid Off?	26
Secret Asian Man	30
Dear Idiot	33
Paper Airplane	36
Another Paper Jam	39
Oh Holy Terror	43
Now, Just in Time for the Holidays	47
Marking My Place	50
Haiti: Humanity in the Humidity	53
The First and Worst Month	57
EXCLUSIVE: Interview with The Yak	59
What I Think They Should Have Called the iPad	63
Remaining Relevant	65
Stalked by a Balloonatic	67
Home Wrecker	69
The One Where I Drive My Mother to the Death Panel at the Local Walmart	73
Filet-O-Feet	77
Get Your Kicks on Route 666	79
In or Out	82

Grow With the Flow 84
Once Bitten, Twice Wry 87
Re-enlisting in the Unemployment Army 90
(And now, a few extras as our free gift to you,
our valued consumer.) 92
Dog Duty 93
Epilogue 98
Colophon 100

Dedication

I **WOULD NEVER** have had the confidence in my own voice had I not listened to every word taught to me by Dr. William Palmer (*http://bit.ly/12Yg6if*) when I was just a teen goof at Alma College. I've been listening to him ever since, even as his name changed simply to Bill. He defines everything a mentor should be—including but not limited to—sending me great writing magazines, sharing jet propelled poetry, giving me the best wordsmith advice even though I stopped paying for it 25 years ago and springing for an occasional Mexican dinner.

And, as always, this too is for The Lady Macraes. God, you three are the salt on my popcorn and the brightest lights of my luminous universe.

Disclaimer or Preface or Author running his mouth off

I'M SORRY ABOUT the title of this book. My buddy assured me it was the best way to get Jon Stewart's or Stephen Colbert's attention. If you first heard of this book on *The Daily Show* or *The Colbert Report*, blimey, it worked! Sadly, you're probably reading this because you're either my mother or the guy out in California who – for reasons unbeknownst to any of us – stole a carton of my books off a loading dock. The paperbacks make for good kindling. Strangely, the Kindle version doesn't.

When I originally wrote this series of essays, ePublications were bright, shiny mysteries. There were no good tools out there for producing tablet versions of books, probably because there were no tablets yet (see Chapter 21, written just before the iPad was announced.) But thanks to the electronic wizardry of publisher John Hile, with the support of editor David Crumm, now all the books from Read The Spirit publications (*http://bit.ly/19dRAav*) are available in all kinds of formats. When Silicon Valley invents a new way to read books, Hile and Crumm will already have a beta version of our books created and uploaded.

You're holding a second edition copy in your hands, whether it's electronic or paperback. There were a few problems with the first edition so if you can track down one of those, it may one day be worth the price you paid for it.

And like I wrote in one of my other books (I sound so cultivated when I say "other books" – I also sound cultivated when I say "cultivated.") I like including videos, hyperlinks, photos and other stuff. The problem is, those gizmos don't really translate too well into paperback form. If you are reading a paperback version, that's where these crazy square symbols come into play. They're QR codes and appear these days on everything from graffiti to tombstones. Scan them with your phone and they take you to a web page or video. This one, I assure you, takes you nowhere near abandoned buildings or grave sites. But go ahead and give 'er a scan; I can wait.

(For those of you on a tablet or who couldn't care less about QR codes, it just goes to my website, www.SpiritualWanderer.com (http://bit.ly/12Yjhqf) where I write up-to-the-minute blogs and probably try to sell you this book. Beware, you could easily find yourself in an infinitely repeating loop.)

Disclaimer or Preface or Author running his mouth off

However you're reading this, I'm glad you bought it (or stole it off a loading dock). Writing it helped me through getting laid off at least twice, possibly three times. But I'm getting ahead of myself, as usual.

CHAPTER **1**

Humor in Hard Times

May, 2009

I knew things weren't good at my company when they closed down half the bathrooms in our building. The economy was going down the toilet, but we sure weren't.

It made me laugh. It shouldn't have though. Still, when everything around you is falling apart, you can either laugh or cry or drink another beer. I've chosen the American way, and am doing all three.

In the past few months, we've been hearing about comparisons between now and the Great Depression. My optimistic side tells me it can be less than two years before this whole mess is over. My pessimistic side points to the entire decade of the 1930s and sighs.

I was heartened to read a report that teens in this country want to know what's going on with the economy and are willing and eager to help their families out. While having this discussion with my wife, my own teen daughter chimed in, "Dad, I can always get a job, you know." She said it with a bit of disgust, but not because of the distaste that employment would bring, but because we hadn't considered that option. Optimistic side: 2 points, Pessimistic: 1.

My buddy points out that this economic collapse can lead to a whole lot more community-building and neighbor-helping-neighbor. My wife thinks that nowadays it's okay and, in fact, important to ask the more personal questions of her friends, "How's your job?" "Everything going okay emotionally?" "Does **your** husband sometimes stare blankly at a computer screen thinking about what to write next?"

Can there be beauty in the breakdown, as the Frou-Frou song (*http://bit.ly/12Yjhqg*) suggests? When the world is running down, can we make the best of what's still around as The Police sing? I guess we won't really know because both groups have split up. Oops, score another one for Pessimism.

I think it's important that we realize we're all in this together (yes, like the Disney song says). Not just in our neighborhood or our city (although one could argue that my town, Detroit, has it really bad), but across the country and indeed the whole planet. And such a globally shared experience is a rare occasion. From Ann Arbor to Addis Ababa, people are going through the same thing.

We're going to make it through this, I tell myself. We have federally insured banks, unlike back in the 30s. We have unemployment pay. And we have the shared memory of our elders who have been through this before. No, we have no idea where it's all headed. But we do know we're a race of humans who put men on the moon, built the Panama Canal, fought off hatred in World War II and created Brangelina.

If we can do all those things, then we can certainly do optimism.

CHAPTER 2

Thoughts Running Through My Head as I'm Getting Laid Off

June, 2009

   Am I getting a gold watch? Wow, the HR lady's kinda hot. Breathe, Rodney, breathe. They all look so sad; make 'em laugh. Ha, they liked the gold watch joke. That guac from the party's gonna go bad if this takes too long. Push Spiritual Wanderer, push Spiritual Wanderer. What does COBRA stand for? Joke about stealing pens. Don't tell 'em about Sharpies. Top boss banters with me about there not being ink in the pens. Phwew, Sharpies are safe. Breathe, breathe, breathe. This is it. This is the end of the career. How long does guacamole last in this heat? Gotta buy a lottery ticket. Seriously, listen to the COBRA spiel. Keep the humor up. Do I hug? If one, then everyone. Top boss reflects on me correcting his tip during our dinner interview three years ago. Says he knew he'd hire me then and there. Should I correct him about something now? They look so serious. Oh, oh, HR lady is nervous; shaky hands give it away. Humor, jokes, feign interest in Employee

Assistance program. Do COBRAs bite or squeeze? Remember to thank sweet daughters for helping me cry earlier so I don't now. Do I sign something? Hey, you forgot to take my ID card. It's ending. Career and this exit interview. Guac's probably a goner too. It's hot. Maybe it's the HR lady. Breathe. Why are they looking at me? Should I say something? Is it my turn to get up and sing? Do I leave? What do I do? Take bull by the horns. Start hugging. Surprises 'em. Ha, hot HR lady says she wants one too.

SCORE!

(Hours later, more Mexican food. Guac's fine.)

CHAPTER 3

Not All Who Wander

July, 2009

I had a bad night a few weeks ago. The kind of night where you wake up thrashing, trapped in sheets from a half-forgotten dream where some part of you still believes it's real. Wakefulness doesn't completely fill the darkness and you're left wondering about the panic. Wondering why you believed the idiocy in your dreams.

Then come the intervening hours trying to fall back asleep.

It was the beginning of our family reunion up in Canada and the full weight of unemployment barged into my nighttime. The money's going to run out, boredom's going to become a barrier between you and your wife, people will stop calling. The void screams at you with silent fears.

It's the kind of night where you beg for clarity from God, dead relatives, any being that happens to be passing by. I was lost for the better part of an hour. Show me a sign; show me something. I prayed for that clarity. I wasn't beyond waking my brother or my mom who were asleep in other parts of the cabin. My immediate family was yet to arrive.

Thankfully, albeit far too slowly, sleep sauntered back and the morning showed up like an extremely tardy dinner guest, brandishing a hot appetizer dish to pass. I pulled on a new favorite shirt, went downstairs to find my bro, his wife and my mother all waiting to take me out to breakfast.

We walked along a small harbor up in Northern Canada and a little yapping dog caught my attention. I strayed over to the sailboat where the noise was coming from and a tiny toy poodle bark, bark, barked at me with its butt wagging like crazy. Soon, on the boat's deck appeared three of them, shouting at me, their owner smiling calmly.

"Can I pet them?" I asked. And of course, with a sail boat load of three piping poodles, there's no way the dogs could be mean or territorial. We got into a chat about where they were from and where they were going, the usual "hi, how are yas."

The boat had a wonderful, pleasant vibe to it and I remarked to my mom, who by now had joined us, that Dad would've loved their lifestyle (the owner having mentioned that he took off from Monroe, Michigan in May and was hoping to be home to carve the

Thanksgiving turkey). Mom reminded me that Dad's retirement goal was to sell the house, buy a boat and live on the high seas.

It was then that I looked carefully at the guy, remembering my rotten sleep hours earlier. Fully looking a stranger over is a bit weird, but something was tugging at me. And there it was; his shirt, albeit a different color and style, said the same thing mine did: 'Not all who wander are lost.'

Okay, it could be a coincidence, sure. And re-reading this story so far it sounds far too much like a Guidepost or Reader's Digest moment. So, add this to the equation: His wife moseys topside to find out what all the barking, laughing and chitchat's about and she too is wearing the same shirt. We laugh about wandering, I naturally plug Spiritual Wanderer (*http://bit.ly/12Yjhqf*), the dogs lick my mom's fingers. I feel better.

I feel a lot, lot better. Maybe it was the over-stuffed breakfast, or the time with my mom, my brother and his wife, or the sunny morning. But my mood isn't that transparent.

Something compelled me to toss on the cool shirt a brother-in-law gave me. Something felt right about finding the boat with the barking dogs and striking up a conversation. Something felt smoother and far more relaxed after the three of us showed up wearing the same slogan.

I'm wearing the shirt now and don't, strangely, feel like taking it off.

CHAPTER **4**

Salivation Army

July, 2009

My family can't wait to hit our local thrift store. They practically drool at the thought of cast-off fashion steals. When I was employed, I felt a little weird about them going to the Salvation Army. Now that I'm not what one would technically call a contributing member of society, I feel fine reaping the harvest of affluent folk's throw-away whims.

One of the first things that greeted me when we walked in the place was a deep discount automatic eyeglass cleaner, marked down a couple times to the bargain basement price of $5.99. I already have one of those though. I call it Kleenex.

There was a buck ninety-nine box of unopened children's Nyquil laying on the floor underneath a hanging row of men's pants. It wasn't as incongruous as the box, costing the same, advertising a Hannah Montana wig. Sadly, the wig was missing and the box was empty.

My daughters, their friend who'd never been there before and my wife wandered over into the girl's and women's fashion section. I could write several paragraphs about their finds but I know intuitively guys wouldn't keep reading. I heard once on TV that if you started a sentence with the phrase "strappy sandals," it would act like a cone of silence and guys would tune out the rest of the conversation.

I'll go as far as mentioning the rack after rack of jean skorts, jean skorts, jean skorts ...

There was an entire wing devoted to red polo shirts. Adult's sizes, kid's sizes, men's and women's. Several of the children's shirts said 'Cress Family Reunion.' Either there was a bad family fallout, a tragic accident or just an overzealous grandma wishing for more kids, but you'd have to have a very specific last name in order to shell out the $3.99 for one of those beauties.

Something far more telling were the sheer volume of Ford, GMC, Dodge, Porsche and Chevrolet red shirts lined up like students at a Vampire Weekend ticket counter. There was even a Legoland shirt in the mix. If shit's going down in Legoland, you **know** the economy's faltering.

Also, for just under five bucks was a Piston's jersey, from our star guard who was traded to the Denver Nuggets. What does it say about me that I found that to be the saddest thing in the joint?

The most expensive item was a framed picture of two clowns playing golf for $34.99. Let's just say I'm saving it for when the Antiques Roadshow comes to town. I have it on good authority that it's an original.

Everything has to have a 99 in the price; I think it's part of their religion. Probably a numerology thing.

I found the Hannah Montana wig over in lamps, right near a Dow Chemical piggy bank. I imagine the conversation going something like "Save your pennies darling and someday soon you can buy your own slutty costume."

(**Editor's note to Disney**: *No, I don't think of Miley Cyrus Incorporated as trashy ... yet!*)

As I was in the checkout aisle with my corralled family—who could've easily spent another hour among the ruins—I heard a guy chatting up the Customer Service desk.

"Yep, I have a hundred-year-old organ," he said.

"Let me take a look at it," she answered.

On my way back to the car I prayed to everything holy that he was talking about a keyboard instrument.

CHAPTER 5

Blatant Attempt to Get on Marketplace

July, 2009

Being a man of infinite shallowness, I often wonder about myself. I wonder why I find such joy in latex. I wonder if I'm abnormal for buying a hand-held "Mister Rogers In Your Pocket (*http://amzn.to/1cZLEIn*)" (complete with sayings like "Please won't you be my neighbor") and leaving it in its original packaging because it's worth more that way. And I wonder if anyone else dreams about somewhat famous radio people like Marketplace's Kai Ryssdal?

We were at a party, Kai and I, and apparently I recognized him from his distinctive voice and started pestering him to say "I'm Kai Ryssdal" the way he says it on air that sort of adds another syllable or two to his first name. I know this isn't normal. Terry Gross or Meeshell Norris sure, but Kai? I'd love to be a commentator on *Marketplace*, so that sort of explains the connection, but I don't really have any expertise in the economy, the

Dow, Ben Bernanke, or the recession, except that it and a faltering newspaper industry laid me off.

I've tried to get noticed by the vast NPR empire and that, too, assuredly makes me a freak. I've sent my book to someone I know at *This American Life* because I think talking to Ira Glass would be freakin' bad-ass. I've written to *On The Media* simply because being laid off *from* the media would qualify me as an expert. *All Things Considered* has most likely taken out a restraining order on me, which probably isn't a bad idea, all things considered. And trust me, if I could somehow write something funny about my Prius, I'd look forward to Click and Clack hanging up on me.

It's not that I'm looking for fame. Okay, yes it is. But I also need to justify my existence these days and make it look like I'm a productive, functioning member of the family. My wife busily works at the computer behind me, editing her various photo shoots and I'm sure she gets tired of me saying "Honey, if you'd just let me join the Navy, there are a zillion jobs for combat photographers." Curiously, 42 results show up with a "combat editors" search at navy.com.

I keep thinking if NPR notices me, then highbrow erudite folks across America would rush to their computers and shell out a tenner for *Spiritual Wanderer*. I'd be safe and secure in my weird little life with my strange proclivities. I wouldn't have to long for the Navy or dream about Garrison Keillor guffawing over something witty I wrote.

Earlier this week, I got a note from a former photojournalism student whose portfolio I critiqued. Apparently I wasn't rude or a total jerk while giving feedback several years ago, unlike some "experts" in the field, and she wanted me to know how sorry she was for what's been happening in the business. It turns out she's a producer at *Marketplace*. I don't know if this will parlay into anything more, but it made me inordinately happy that karma is alive and at play.

    Looking for a conclusion, and thinking the above paragraph comes close but not close enough, I naturally looked to America's favorite neighbor, Fred Rogers. He tells me it's a beautiful day in my neighborhood and that discovering truth will make me free. Sadly, he doesn't provide Carl Kasell's phone number.

CHAPTER 6

Cost Saving Tips

August, 2009

I'm not so sure the cable lady bought my story about being recently laid off. She was sympathetic to my cause when I called asking for a break on my monthly rate. But when I asked for another high definition DVR and a faster Internet connection she had to "go ask her boss." Still, when the deal was done I had both of my requests filled and a whopping two bucks in monthly savings.

The recession has its benefits.

They're serving pizza next Tuesday at the area Shield's Pizzerias (*http://bit.ly/TV339o*) and if you're unemployed, you get a free pie. I'm wondering how they check. Since I haven't received the barcode tattoo yet from the Michigan Unemployment Agency there's nothing for them to scan so perhaps it's on the honor system. I'm of two minds—three actually. The only thing I love more than pizza is *free* pizza. But if it means having to admit to a waitress that the family sitting in front of

her isn't worth what they used to be, I'm not so sure I want to eat humble pizza pie. That, and I've been losing weight ever since I got laid off. Do I really want to jinx the process with pepperoni?

We've shut off the sprinkler system for our lawn. It's been a cooler than normal summer so my grass isn't as brown as it could be. Besides, a green lawn just seems so ostentatious these days. Where are we living, a country club? I figure August eventually will come to an end and the rains will become more frequent. Besides, maybe this will kill those pesky weeds that seem to spring up first when the ground's wet.

Sure, I *could* stop drinking those darn Cappuccino Blasts. But there are certain inalienable rights in this country and that delectable concoction is one of them. They'll get my frozen coffee when they pry it outta my cold, dead hands. Yes, they're smaller in size lately, but that's due to my aforementioned weight loss and not our family financials. I have my priorities.

Did I mention I'm now morally and ethically clean if I shop at Walmart? Yes indeed. Whereas in the past I turned up my nose at $1.99 Life cereal because of their anti-union policies and small business busting practices, now I hold my head high as I greet their greeters and wish *them* a nice day. I still feel a bit dirty shopping there, but it's a fun dirty.

And lastly, I'm letting others pick up the tab at meals. Granted, most of the time it's my mom, but I've been swallowing my pride, along with the free lunches or dinners that friends slash family have offered to pay for. In the past, I always reached for my wallet. I still reach for it, but in a fake way now. It's like I have to pretend I'm going to pay even though we both know I won't. It's diabolical.

I'm looking forward to hanging with my lifelong buddy in Ann Arbor tomorrow to watch some pre-season football. He mentioned getting some pizza and plopping in front of the tube. I can guarantee he'll pay even though I'll pretend otherwise. Maybe a veggie pizza will fit his bottom line and my waistline.

CHAPTER 7

Until Now, I've Never Lied on My Resume

August, 2009

    I have several different versions of my resume out circulating. I decided to share my acting resume that I drew up when I signed on with a local talent agency to try and break into all these locally produced movies around town. So far I've had a few nibbles, but I'm waiting for Judd Apatow or Leslie Mann to officially invite me over for pizza. I think I'd hold my own after getting over that little awkward part about me having absolutely no experience in the field. They seem like such a cool family and even their daughters act. They remind me of someone; I just can't place it though.

Here's the actual resume I sent in:

- I was the nerd they kept shoving into *The Hurt Locker*.
- I was a cuticle in *Seussical*.
- I got my start as the anal-retentive little boy who wouldn't squeeze the Charmin toilet paper.
- I played the third option in *Sophie's Choice*.
- I helped develop a script with Peter O'Toole about the WWI misadventures of a Caribbean anti-hero called Lawrence of Aruba
- I was the 13th Angry Man but was cut due to superstitions surrounding that number.
- I came up with the rules for *Fight Club,* but I'm not allowed to talk about them.
- I directed Grape Expectations, the prequel to *Raisin in the Sun*.
- Whenever the Coen boys see me they exclaim in unison, "O Brother."

CHAPTER 8

Goaded by My Goatee

August, 2009

Poking out from my chin and jawbones, my whiskers belie my age. Whereas my head hair is mostly the same color it was back in my obnoxious seventh grade portrait—the one where upon seeing it Heidi Obenhoff said, "Oh, you look nice," which to this date is the biggest lie anyone's ever told me—my face hair is more salt than pepper.

On this Labor Day weekend I've decided not to shave. It wasn't an act of solidarity with my unemployed brethren; 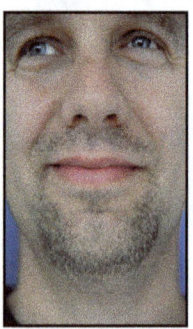 it was simply laziness. Besides, I don't know if I'm unemployed anymore. I have a date with a woman at the Michigan Works office to find out if my status has changed or not. Unlike on Facebook, changing my status requires paperwork and the potential to lose a ton of cash.

I am working a few days a week now as a visiting or adjunct or part-time professor in the Journalism Department at Michigan State University. So far, so good, and I can't believe how excited I am to teach. The problem is, I am making about a sixth of what I made at the Detroit Free Press. Does that disqualify me for unemployment benefits and will I be wiped clean from their rosters? Or will the government dole supplement my professorial pay?

That's what I hope to find out on my date. It's one of the reasons dates are so exciting; you never know if you'll get lucky in the end.

I'll shave my goatee by then. Hell, it'll be gone by the time I return to class tomorrow; I don't want to scare the students. But it just amazes me how there are certain signs that pop up on my way to my previously perceived apocalypse: age 50. Face it, literally, I'm on the gray side of 40. But there's nothing like a few fast-growth hairs on my chinny-chin-chin to tell me I'm not as young as I used to be.

But age has its benefits as I heard, I think, in some commercial a long time ago. With age I can tell the students thousands of stories from my two-dozen-plus years in the field. I can give them advice and read their stories with a fair amount of confidence that what I'm telling them is true and as good for them as spinach or aerobics. Also, with age, I don't have to worry as much if they're enjoying themselves. Teaching these classes a few years ago I would've worried if they liked me or were having a good time. Today, sure, I care about that, but honestly my biggest concern is, "Am I giving them enough work to do?"

That's how you know you've crossed over. You don't need cotton-colored facial hair to tell you that. When you spend excess energy concerned your students will not learn enough if they don't get enough homework, you are coming dangerously close to becoming that old curmudgeon you used to laugh about when you were little. "Hey you kids, get off my lawn!"

My beard is my picture of Dorian Gray. It ages in the hidden confines of my attic until I forget to shave. My until-now secret fear of clowns doesn't have such a telltale sign. Neither does my irrational fear of spilling things, unless you count the weird overreaction that takes place every time I get nudged or bumped while carrying something to drink.

But beards don't lie.

The informer dies at sunrise.

CHAPTER 9

Marvin and Me

September, 2009

    My buddy Marvin just hung up on me. I should probably clarify; MARVIN spells his name with all capital letters and he's not really my buddy. He pretends to be Michigan's Automated Response Voice Interactive Network, but that's just a charade. When I phone him, I hear a male voice. That is, up until he asks a question I can't answer, or worse, I have a question he's ill equipped to deal with. He's ill equipped for a lot these days.

    When you're laid off, you are entitled to something called, in layman's terms, money. That money is supposed to come from a state agency that subsidizes your pay to the tune of, oh I don't know, one-tenth of what you made in real life. You'll get your money but I think you need to buy Marv a beer or at least talk about the Lions with him. Somehow you have to get yourself on his good side so he doesn't hang up on you. I've been trying to figure out, for quite some time now, if accepting a job as an adjunct professor at Michigan State University was going to disqualify me for unemployment cash. No one I've spoken with knows for sure. Even though I'm now making a sixth of what I made at the Free Press, the paychecks haven't started arriving and won't, I'm told, for weeks. So does that sixth come out of the tenth I'd be making on unemployment or is it supplemental or … (suddenly my head starts to ache and I say very unkind things to my computer screen and, by default, my patient wife sitting behind me at her terminal).

Marty, or Merv or whatever his name is hung up on me when I couldn't answer whether or not I made any money for the first few weeks of September. "Okay," I wanted to ask, but was given no option, "does that mean did I work during those weeks even though payment should arrive sometime before Halloween, or how do you define making money, Mark?" (I figure I won't go to the trouble of learning his name if he won't afford me common telephonic courtesy).

When you get hung up on these days, it's just no fun hanging back up on them. The call goes dead and there's no cradle to slam the phone down in, you just have to be satisfied with angrily pushing the END button with your thumb, but I did it with vehemence, so I think that counts for style points.

I honestly don't know how people figure the system out. I'm college educated—hell I'm a college professor—and I can't make sense of where the money comes from or, more importantly, *if* it comes to me.

At some point in the not-too-distant future, MARVIN and I may bury the hatchet and talk to each other like rational human beings, or at least like rational voice mail robots and human beings. He may have to make the first move though. Offer me some playoff tickets to the Tigers, or show up with a basketball tucked under his arm asking to shoot some hoop, perhaps.

He'll have to apologize for his rude behavior. And somehow he'll have to answer if he considers me a loser or not, since when I'm being completely honest with myself, that's really what this is all about, deep down.

CHAPTER **10**

Laid Back or Laid Off?

September, 2009

When I got a phone call from my buddy Ryan Wood (*http://bit.ly/188lVb3*) and he couldn't stop laughing, I knew something was up. He told me I had a "double truck" in the latest NPPA (*http://www.nppa.org/*) magazine. Normally, a photographer gets excited by something like that because it means he scored a big display space, showing one of his photos across two pages.

Oh how wrong could I have been! They ran **ME** across two pages. Maybe my wife could be excited, not due to seeing me clothed and in the tub, but because it's her photo.

As of this writing, the magazine has yet to arrive at my door, due to historically incomprehensibly bad mail service here. But, I've seen a camera phone version sent to me by the Director of Photography at USA Today (*http://usat.ly/188lVb6*), Mick Cochran. I've been razzed about it in front of my class and I've even been asked pointed questions about where the staples went in.

Anyway, I thought I'd share the layout above and the story that accompanied it below.

Life In Layoff Land

By Rodney Curtis

I've carried a dark secret buried inside me throughout my photojournalism career. No, it's not that I'm colorblind. That's a given if you've seen me try and tone anything that's not natural daylight. No, my secret is far more nefarious. I was a closet writer. I say *was* because last year I finally got a book published and the cat's outta the Domke.

My secret almost slipped out when, in 1987 at my Flint Journal internship, I was scheduled to work a rainy Sunday afternoon when nothing was going on. I was supposed to look for features but instead stayed in the office and wrote a three-page excuse to my boss, complete with quotes and dialog from an imagined cop and recalcitrant hooker. Jayson Blair would've been so proud!

(Note to shooters: recalcitrant means defiant of authority)

During my two dozen years in the business, first as a photog then as an editor, I always gravitated towards the writers, palling up with whoever I loved reading. It always bothered me though when they'd say, "You know photographers. They can't spell worth a darn and their captions …"

I hated being stereotyped. Not only wasn't it true for me, it isn't true for many photojournalists out there who can write something fierce.

I shot for the Ann Arbor News and the Concord Monitor. I shared a job with my wife at AP. And I hopped over to editing at the Midland Daily News, Detroit News and finally the Detroit Free Press. The entire time I tried to slip in a story here and a very, very, very extended cutline there.

My fantastic boss at the Midland Daily News, Jack Telfer, said he hired me because of my cover letter. They let me fly my freak flag up there and I wrote columns, editorial opinion, even stories. My favorite being the one about the little old lady who cracked open an egg and no yolk came out. I went over to her house with my cool Leica feeling like a bad-ass documentarian. She opened the margarine container and showed me the egg she saved. I went back and whipped up a story omelet complete with a dozen egg facts. I still remember her lift quote, "It was a queer chicken that laid that egg."

Then came the layoff from the Free Press. I was politely but firmly told I was no longer needed around the place and that I should probably get along home now. Since I thought it would be too ballsy to snap pictures during the actual layoff and hiding a microphone somewhere on my person took too much effort I just figured I'd write a stream of consciousness piece about what was going on inside my head at the time.

It's gotten some publicity around the web and now it resides in a place I like to call Layoff Land. I've parked it there along with other musings—some funny, some serious, (but mostly funny) about what it's like to no longer be a real journalist. You can find it and sample chapters from my book at www.SpiritualWanderer.com (*http:// bit.ly/188lSfr*).

Life as a recovering photo editor isn't as bad as I feared. My family and my words give me something to do. I should be downstairs watching High School Musical 3 with my kids but instead I've snuck up here to my laptop to beg all of you not to be fearful about the future. Find your passion, even if it's still photography and don't let go of it. Sure, you may have to do other things to make money since we can't rely on newspapers to hire us. I have a kick-ass resume right now if I wanted to get a job at a paper in 1999.

But it's not as bad as it seems. The sun still rises and sets and the color shifts still give me fits. I can do this. Like Gloria Gaynor, I will survive.

Although, honestly, ask me again in another month or so when my severance runs out.

CHAPTER 11

Secret Asian Man

October, 2009

I'm not sure if I'm playing hooky from Chinese school right now or if I've done my duty to its fullest and received a gold star by my name. Only time will tell.

Back when the Olympics were held in Beijing, my oldest daughter had a bunch of Chinese friends; one of which made plans to take her back home during the summer and spend time watching gymnastics or pole vaulting or whatever tickets they could get. The problem was, my daughter didn't speak the language, so everybody thought maybe a quick tutorial would be in order.

We had no idea a primer on the Chinese language would turn into three years of Saturday school and our eventual forced volunteering. Beijing never happened. Well, the Olympics did, but my daughter and her friend fell out of each other's favor and then the girl moved away. However, since Skye, my eldest, was enjoying the process of learning a completely incomprehensible foreign tongue, we ponied up the tuition and let her keep going.

And then the email arrived. We think it came earlier this week but since our spam filter, for some crazy reason, sifted out characters that it didn't recognize, this may have been its third or ninth mailing. A synopsis of the bulletin, when we got through the wacky translation, was that we, as parents, were expected to show up this Saturday and offer up our services. Several back and forth notes flew and we finally nailed down that we were just supposed to report to the office for instructions.

Okay, so half an hour ago I wandered around the local middle school, which had been taken over for the day. Ignoring the middle-aged men walking the halls with swords (I never figured that one out), I realized the normal office, where secretaries and principals stay, wasn't where the Chinese school worked out of. I finally found the janitor's closet where they'd set up shop and reported for "duty."

The woman racing around seemed to realize I was a fish out of its aquarium and pointed at a large sandwich board sign that needed to be set up outside. I wasn't sure exactly where, so I made up a place that looked official and put it down. It was all in Chinese, I assume, and they could've said anything from "No Parking" to "Kick this guy; he's a moron."

After that, I reported back to the closet and she pointed to two more signs. I was to take these upstairs and set them up at the end of each hallway. "QUIET" was written on the bottom after a long series of characters. I put them up amidst the clatter and chatter of parents and students rushing around me. I can only guess they said something like, "This is a test. Let's see if this dad tries to make you all QUIET."

I never figured out what my role was. Hopefully, it was just to place the signs and leave. I went back down and found the woman in charge and she handed me a clipboard filled with Chinese words, or names, or bus schedules and the only thing I recognized was **Rodney**. That, and I *think* I saw the character for Kung Pao chicken, but I'm not certain.

Apparently, I had to sign it to prove I was there. The irony didn't escape me. During my work week I'm a university professor who is charged, among other things, with taking attendance. And yet here, in this closet, I had to sign in to show that I had moved four signs into place.

I think the woman told me I could go up to my daughter's class, but since the hall outside was filled with the second-grader's parents (my 15-year-old is that advanced!), I wasn't really sure what use I'd be or even if I was allowed in.

So I left. Hopefully the men in sweats and swords won't come after me.

I'll go get her in another hour or so and will be truly bummed if there's some cold carryout Kung Pao chicken waiting for me that I missed.

CHAPTER 12

Dear Idiot

October, 2009
(I wrote the following note to a Michigan member of Congress after he made an inflammatory and fact-less speech about health care. After filling out all the fields on his website and carefully typing it in, they rejected it because I'm not in his district. Thanks Congressman! Way to listen to the people of Michigan.)

Dear Congressman,

In your opening remarks on the health care debate you quoted some very suspicious statistics. Where do you get your information from? According to the non-partisan Families USA (*http://bit.ly/188lSft*), nearly 90 million people—about one-third of the population below the age of 65 spent a portion of either 2007 or 2008 without health coverage. You said 85 percent of Americans have health care. Those of us struggling to pay $1,000 per month for health care are jealous of your mythic 85 percenters.

According to the study you quoted in your opening remarks before Congress, you claim that under the British and Canadian system, cancer survival rates are worse than those in the US. Please Congressman, the study clearly states it's the *under privileged* and *poor folks* in Britain that are less likely to survive cancer, not the population as a whole. The same is true in our country under our current, for lack of a better word, "*plan.*" The study went on to conclude that less affluent members of society are "less pushy" and less confident when it came to their dealings with their health service, therefore they were less inclined to use said health service. This meant that when their cancer was finally diagnosed, it would be at a later stage, making it more difficult to treat and lowering the likelihood of survival. Maybe you didn't read the study.

I'm guessing you didn't read it, or you had an aide do so because the study went on to conclude survival rates have increased to record levels almost across the board, thanks to new treatments and greater awareness. The researchers concluded that if the gap between rich and poor patients was closed, the net result would be 3,000 less cancer deaths per year.

Shame on you Congressman. You are resorting to old and tired scare tactics by saying women won't have as great a chance surviving breast cancer under the plan being considered by Democrats. That is plain demagoguery. There may be people in the country who believe your spin, but using statistics about poor people in a British system is either mean or dumb. I'm wondering which one you are.

And let's get something else straight. Did you or didn't you read the plans under consideration? I've seen a video of you saying you read them, adding that they were too boring to read. Hmm, which was it?

Do you really believe that the government should stay out of health care? If so, I think the millions of people on Medicare and Medicaid would thank you for your compassionate conservatism.

I am a laid off worker in your home state of Michigan. I sincerely hope you do a lot better with your facts in the future. We here in the Great Lake State expect better from our elected officials. And by the way, my wife and daughters and I hope you're enjoying your wonderful government-allocated health plan that protects you and your loved ones.

Sincerely,
Rodney Curtis

CHAPTER **13**

Paper Airplane

November, 2009

  I'm little in this story. I can't even be old enough for kindergarten. A quickly folded paper airplane I've created flies into the cold, drafty fireplace in our Pleasant Ridge living room and since this is a time before energy efficient enclosures and fake, crackly logs I remove the screen and grab my plane. I flinch, and ash from a long dormant fire flicks up into my right eye and stings.
  As all good mothers were doing back in the 1960s, mine was in the kitchen or cleaning or talking with Mrs. Lockerbie next door and I ran to her crying about the pain. It was a simple procedure, washing the ash from around my eye and splashing water into my face while explaining I had to fight the instinctual blinking. Routine, yet I was devastated. I was afraid I was going to "be on the news."
  Vietnam was always the talk of the black and white men in suits on TV. Either that or the riots in Detroit or

some political leader who my parents liked was getting shot. Bad things happened on the news. That's where the men with somber faces told everyone about the sad stuff. God, I was going to be reported on.

I still remember Mom's face as her eyes twinkled and she shook her head slowly side to side. "No honey, you won't be on the news." It was such a huge relief. The pain had only lasted an instant, but the fear of being exposed lasted what seemed like hours longer, even though it couldn't have even been minutes.

I think of that incident these days as I teach my students literary journalism. They bring in stories they've found or ones they've written and always, always their words are fascinating, fun, factual and well-written. It's news but it's so very far from the kind I grew up watching on a blurry 12-inch diagonal screen.

News then was about bad things. News today is about everything.

Kids today *want* to be in the news. It bothered me when I was in the field shooting pictures all the time. They would say, "take my picture," or the less observant ones would yell, "put me on TV," even though my camera looked nothing like a video recorder. They want to be recognized or noticed. It's so much healthier than back when we feared even watching anything anywhere close to six o'clock.

I think I've conquered that long-ago fear. And either I'm suffering from severe Stockholm Syndrome or I've greatly progressed since my news-fearing days. I'm part of the news establishment now, even teaching it to college students. The campus radio station has asked me to read more of my stories on air and I look forward to it with delight instead of dread.

And somehow, inexplicably, I'm getting sucked back into the dance again as two rich brothers—who got their start back exactly when this story did—have decided to form a new newspaper in the area and they've asked me to photo edit the endeavor.

My paper airplane flies again. And yes, here comes the metaphor. The folds are more engineered and my aim is far better than it was. But mostly, I don't fear the ashes anymore.

CHAPTER **14**

Another Paper Jam

November, 2009

    For one brief moment, I was back in the game. I could smell the ink and newsprint as the papers rolled off the presses. I found myself eating carryout off my lap as I drove to the next assignment. While shooting random features I connected with an oldster, a hipster and an anonymous weightlifter whom I shot through a workout window as he hoisted barbells in silhouette.

    Then, like any former addiction, the *NEW*spaper experiment ended abruptly, leaving me without my drug of choice, journalism. I've described myself as a recovering photo editor. That seems apropos since the inevitable highs and lows that come with newspapering are much like any addictive substance.

I found myself excited about the possibilities, loving the photo editing process, grooving on being with fellow shooters and seeing my shots in print. But along with those highs came the caffeine diet, the irregular sleep, the frustration with management and the complaining. Even being in the newsroom for less than two weeks, the complaining—mine included—was substantial. We journalists call it bitching. Sorry, journalists call it that. I'm not really a journalist anymore.

I probably should've listened to my gut.

As this new venture, started by two rich retired brothers, came into my consciousness, a part of me rebelled at the prospect of getting back into the fray. The first few meetings I took, over breakfast with the initial editor, left me feeling ambiguous and hesitant. I found myself happy that the paper was delayed once, then again, then a third time. In the ensuing months I became a teacher and felt as though I'd found my calling, or my calling had found me. Neither one of us knew the other was looking.

You can tell when your calling is calling. Things like—I don't know—you feel excited about the opportunities and don't dread going into work. There was tons of ambiguity in teaching. I didn't even know what literary journalism was until Google told me. I still don't have the promised class syllabus they said they'd share with me, so I make it up as I go along. *(Note to any of my students who may have unwittingly stumbled upon this story: the previous sentence was only for comedic effect).*

(Note to the rest of you: not really.)

In this latest newspaper incarnation though, the ambiguity made me irrationally mad. Whereas at Michigan State University when they answered my "how do

I get my email" request with "we put it in a mail slot in the copier room," I just laughed and shared the story with the class. At the Detroit Daily Press my anger flared when there wasn't any soap, or when there was, but then there weren't any towels in the men's room.

It seems my family is happy to have me back. Even if I'm not adding money to the coffers. Christmas won't be—how shall we say—overly extravagant this year, but the crazy enigmatic smile on my daughter's face when she heard the paper closed after only five days of publication said it all. There was good and bad in that smile. Mostly good though. She just didn't want to overly show how gleeful she was that Mr. Grumpy Puss had gone into hibernation and possible extinction.

Yeah, I have all these pictures I shot during a 5:00 a.m. Black Friday assignment and no place to put them. That weightlifter I stalked won't ever see publication and to the hipster woman with the dog in the sling, I still love

Black Friday at Partridge Creek Mall in Clinton Twp.

the idea of your blind and deaf dog visiting school children. Call me, won't you?

Man, losing two newspaper jobs in less than half a year? That's the stuff of Guinness, (the beer or the book, your pick).

CHAPTER **15**

Oh Holy Terror

December, 2009

Watching the new *3D IMAX Christmas Carol,* I kept wondering what it would be like to take off in my time machine, snatch the original author and plop him down in the mostly empty seats next to me just to get his reaction. It would probably scare the Dickens out of him.

I guess I didn't realize, in my grownup years, how frightening that story really is. In *IMAX* and in *3D* you may as well leave your toddlers at home. Your teens too. It's no wonder Johnny Mathis includes it (*http://bit.ly/188lVbb*) as the one drawback in his *Most Wonderful Time of the Year* standard. "There'll be scary ghost stories and tales of old gories ..." although I may be mishearing the lyrics.

Visages from beyond the grave have always been popular. These days, movies involving the undead seem to need something campy or wry as a hook. Isn't the fact that dead people have come back from the grave and are walking around like fans at Ford Field enough of a weird twist, or have we come to expect something more showy from our animated dead bodies? More magical? More abra cadaver?

I was wondering if there was any connection between Christmas and zombies so of course, I immediately thought of Jesus. But his epic tale of rising from the dead happened at Easter. This is his birthday we're celebrating on the 25th, or is it Target's? You certainly can't tell by the advertisements.

It was then that I stumbled upon It's Beginning to Look a Lot Like Zombies: A Book Of Zombie Christmas Carols (*http://bit.ly/188lVbc*). Author Michael P. Spradlin shares his lyrics to yuletide standards like, *We Three Spleens, Good King Wenceslas Tastes Great, Have Yourself a Medulla Oblongata* and my favorite, *Deck The Halls With Parts of Wally.*

Maybe it's due to the holiday's proximity to Halloween. We run the gauntlet from frightening to fa-la-la in less than two months. Without Charles Dickens, would Christmastime be a lot less scary? I don't know, Santa would still stalk children all year, knowing when they've been good or peed their pants in school. He'd still break into their homes if, and only if, the children were asleep. And lest we forget those claymation spectacles back in the day featuring all those nasties trying to keep Christmas from happening. And oh that bitch, The Grinch!

My daughters conquered any real or imagined Santa fears by trying to trap him with cleverly placed bubble wrap on the floor around the Christmas tree. I remember just being creeped out when I was little by the jolly old elf at a Christmas tree lot who kept motioning at me to come over and get a candy cane from him. Didn't Mom and Dad warn me about taking candy from a stranger? Clowns did the same thing for my vague anxieties.

So if you're not hiding under your parent's coffee table as the "holiday classics" are playing on TV, and if you've gotten past your fear of the cat burglar dressed all in red from his head to his foot, then maybe you have a fighting chance at rejoicing or being merry. But that's a lot of noelphobia to overcome.

There's always the real-life shopping zombies, too, on the night before Christmas. That was the night, no joke, when several years ago I was stumbling through Walgreens with my father-in-law and pointed out a Foreman Grill in an opened box and lurched for it instinctively. Here's the conversation as best I can remember it:

"Hey, I can get that for Chelsea, (my sister-in-law)."
"She's a vegetarian," said my father-in-law.
"Maybe she can grill vegetables on it."
"I don't know how much use she'd get out of it."
"Well, she could return it and get what she wants."

Thankfully, we left the store with only—I don't know—bottled wassail or eggnog or some last minute thing we *really* needed.

There are enough real-world things to be scared of at Christmas: a lackluster economy, elves making toys in Singapore sweatshops and retail sales cooler than the North Pole. We don't need to go adding the Winter Warlock or the mean Burgermeister Meisterburger (*http://bit.ly/12YjhGB*) into the equation. Although those zombie carols are pretty funny, I must admit.

But for those of you who simply must scare yourself this holiday season and don't seem to be freaked out by the 40 old white Republican Senators deciding health care for the other hundred million of us (I'm not saying they're zombies, but I'm not sayin' they ain't), then check out this list of the Top 10 Christmas Horror Movies (*http://bit.ly/12YjfhT*). My favorite title being Santa Claws: His Slay Bells are ringing! No, I haven't seen any

of them and don't plan to. If Rudolph's Abominable Snowman makes me uneasy how am I supposed to deal with Santa's Slay (*http://imdb.to/12YjfhV*)?

CHAPTER **16**

Now, Just in Time for the Holidays

December, 2009
   Carbon Offsets for Sale
   Yes, you too can feel like you're giving something back this holiday season when you purchase your officially sanctioned Spiritual Wanderer (*http://amzn.to/12YjhGG*) carbon offsets. Why let the world leaders in Copenhagen have all the fun when you can easily participate in the purchasing of genuine carbon offsets for your business or home?

   Here's how it works: As opposed to sending all your hard-earned dollars (or Blu-ray players), to some third world country that wouldn't appreciate them, send them to me. Say you own a factory, or even just drive a large, gas-guzzling SUV. For a mere fraction of your monthly costs, you can pay me—an unemployed American—to *drive my dogs and Prius* around the economically ravaged suburbs of Detroit. I could go see a carbon-neutral movie, fill up with some greenhouse gas, or even drive to Michigan State University (whose colors are green and white), to lecture my former students about harmful emissions.

If you send me enough to fill up my tank (a mere $15–$20), I'll send you a certificate saying you're a good steward of the planet, have treated Mother Earth with respect and I'll even throw in a trip to the recycling center in your honor. That's not all. Since the climate talks focus on hard to understand concepts like cap and trade, global warming, the Kyoto Protocol and Al Gore, I'll send the first 100 responders several invaluable web links to places that explain such terminology. What a great stocking stuffer!

Just think of little Timmy's eyes when he opens up his specially wrapped offset, "Gee Dad, can we apply it to our Hummer right now?"

Why, yes you can, little buckaroo. But that's not all. If you order before midnight, I'll throw in an official screen shot of your order, taken directly from my enviro-friendly LED-powered monitor. Sorry gang, I'd love to send you a paper certificate but how eco-cool is that? Not very.

You may be wondering if your money will be wisely spent, or if it will just be used to produce even more harmful gases. That's a valid concern, so let me assure you that unlike the delegates in Denmark, who are arriving via those nasty airplanes and stretch limos, your money will only be used to power my 2005 Prius, which I purchased used, from a locally owned and operated dealership right here in Michigan. If I slip up and happen to purchase a Cappuccino Blast with your offset money, I will most certainly recycle all or most of the cup.

And just to show how serious I am about recycling, let me recycle a joke from the previous chapter: "Isn't the fact that dead people have come back from the grave and are walking around like fans at Ford Field enough of a weird twist or have we come to expect something more showy from our animated dead bodies? More magical? More abra cadaver?"

Despite what idiot conservatives think, global warming is real. And so are my carbon offsets. Order now and avoid the Christmas, er, holiday rush. Your mother will thank you. Mother Earth that is. Ho, ho, ho.

CHAPTER **17**

Marking My Place

January, 2010
My bookmark tells me how much money I'm saving by being unemployed. It's not a webpage bookmark but an actual, two-dimensional slip of paper with pen scrawlings like *minus $110.22 for union dues* or *negative $30 for parking*. I keep that slip wedged between the incongruous pages of Eat, Pray, Love (*http://bit.ly/12Y-jhGL*) to remind me of the feelings I had before going under the knife.

The vague, yet constant fear of losing two dozen years' worth of credibility was only slightly less gut-clenching than the evaporation of a salary, 401K and insurance. That bookmark, done up in classic Rodney MBLSP style, (*management by little slips of paper*), kept reassuring me that my costs would also go down the toilet with my job. City of Detroit taxes would be no more, as would the five weekly lunches which I used more as an escape from the insanity than as nourishment.

I like looking at the bookmark now because that Rodney guy seems remote and cold. There's something about him though, that I just can't place. I try to go back inside his head and feel the vibe from time to time. I don't do this metaphorically or metaphysically, I actually try to re-connect with him and see what went so wrong.

And then today I had lunch with some friends who still work in the business and I caught a quick passing glimpse of myself. He didn't notice me, which every science fiction writer will tell you is lucky—butterfly effect and all. But it was in the face of someone I met while downtown before meeting my friends. He is sitting very near where I used to sit, along that strange limbo lane near Layoff Land. And in seeing him, whether it was my proximity near my former job, or the similarities between us, it all came rushing back.

The sense of abandonment by people I worked with daily. The inability to fully engage in a conversation that wasn't about the newspaper's future. The panic about being the breadwinner. The anger over being targeted for dismissal. And the restless shiftiness I felt I was portraying. It's nearly impossible to do your job when you are forced to have irons in other fires because you have it on good authority that your own fire is about to be doused.

I saw that in my former co-worker's face and it made me sad. He was me.

There's no earthly reason why I should be feeling so much better now than I did then. When I received confirmation this morning that another three hundred and something was heading directly into my account from the state unemployment agency, there's no explanation for why I threw both my hands into the air fists first. My contentment with my incoming funds doesn't make sense on a rational level when, like my laptop battery, they currently rest at about 29% of their former capacity.

And yet I lie here, belly flopped on my bed first, then doing the backstroke. All the while my cursor asks me with a slash or a sideways enigmatic pursed lip, "Are you sure you want to tell them this?"

I blink back at my cursor, not fearing its curses, and tell it, "yeah."

Life out here after the apocalypse is actually better for me than before all the bombs dropped. Money never was everything. And now that it's closer to nothing than everything, I've realized there are so many more bookmarks to tell me where I am. To keep me in place and remind me where to return to.

You can catch a break on your taxes and you can quit eating out all the time. You can see if the cable people will cut you a deal and you should *always, always, always* look in the radically reduced section of your grocer's meat shelves. Tonight we had marinated filet mignon simply because Kroger felt it should've been sold already.

You've probably seen through my charade. You've probably guessed I'm not writing this for me. That's very astute of you. Many of you reading this are journalists—including you, my friend, whom I met today. "Yeah," like I said to my cursor. I'm writing this to you.

CHAPTER **18**

Haiti: Humanity in the Humidity

January, 2010
(The following story was originally published early in 1994 after I went on a self-assignment to Haiti. With the horrible earthquake last week I keep thinking about my brief stay on the island 17 years ago.)

I can't really say why I went down to Haiti in the first place. Ron, a priest friend of mine, wrote and suggested I make the journey to see some places and faces that would fill a whole book. Like every egocentric photographer, that was all I really needed to hear.

"Sure," I thought, "I'd love to have a million images to choose from. And my portfolio could stand to have a little third-world poverty thrown in to give it that caring, humanist look."

I was such a jerk.

When *National Geographic* said they'd like to see what I came back with, I was hooked. Yeah, I was curious about the country and being nosy makes me a good journalist. But these motivations for making the journey were about as shallow as the fresh water ponds found on the island and just as slimy.

As my plane was taking off from Miami I realized I was just this side of clueless. I was between jobs and didn't have a long time to prepare for this. Plus, I was just getting adjusted to the thought of becoming a new daddy. My wife and I heard the news just days before my trip.

In preparation, I had learned a little Haitian history and some details about the political climate, but I spent zero time learning about the people and studying their language. It was sheer willpower that stayed my nerves and forced me to get off the plane in Port-au-Prince. Heat, it was a blast furnace during summer. After worming through customs and haggling for a good taxi fare, I found myself winding through a Caribbean hell. I was driving in comparative luxury in a battered old pickup truck with a driver who looked to be about 90 years old. Streets that would have been happier lining Mogadishu carried us past the pre-teenage hookers gesturing suggestively, the dilapidated shanties that housed several families and the frightening sight of children bathing in sewage. But they couldn't carry us far enough away from the smell; a sickly sweet, sour scent that sticks to you and works its way inside your soul.

After Ron took me to his mission that doles out food, water and medical attention (no, they don't try to convert the residents), I started to understand the mood and rhythm of Haiti. I was told that everyone wears long pants on the weekdays and shorts on the weekends. I wanted to fit in. I wanted it to appear that the humidity wasn't affect me, so I pulled on some jeans and a bulky photo vest. I stuck out like an accountant at a nudist resort. Everywhere we walked, we heard the cry, "Blanc, Blanc!" meaning, "Hey look, it's a white guy."

Once we were visiting a clinic in the worst section of town, Cité Soleil, and suddenly the military showed up and began dragging a young man away. Our driver told me to get into the van and stop taking pictures. He was frightened for his life as well as ours. I had to watch as a woman ran out pleading for the soldiers not to take her son away. The army had our van surrounded and even if I didn't have the nerve to shoot them, I'm sure they would have had the nerve to shoot me.

The next day we were in an orphanage, which had a strict rule against photography. So a doctor I was traveling with told me to just hang out and play with the kids. I chose a room with some of the younger children and sat on the concrete floor. Soon, the nun attending the room left and I had 15 young waifs running in, dancing, running out and just playing the silly kid games that every nationality and race plays. As the action began to move outside, I noticed a few tinier ones weren't participating, so I stayed indoors with them. They were the ones I earlier tried to keep from being bullied due to their size. I waved them over and they lay down in my lap and, amazingly, fell fast asleep. One of the girls woke 10 or 15 minutes later and went out to play but one little girl with straggly hair, dirty cotton dress and tired old eyes stayed cuddled in my lap, drinking in the contact and affection.

My doctor friend came by and kneeled down next to me. Looking over the tiny girl asleep in my lap, he gently informed me she had AIDS and probably wouldn't grow up to be a normal, healthy child.

My heart melted in the Haitian heat. All that little girl wanted out of life was a few moments of sanctuary in my lap. God, I wanted to rescue her and bring her back home. If my wife hadn't been pregnant with our own baby daughter, there's no telling how far I would've pushed the adoption process. I think it was then that I finally realized my trip wasn't pointless.

It wasn't all about photography. It had something to do with participating instead of observing. Seeing the man dragged from the slums to almost certain death was important even if my camera didn't capture the image. Feeling the little girl's need as she clung to my lap was never recorded with lens or film but nevertheless was etched on my soul.

Thank goodness I was able to put the camera down in times like those and pick up my humanity.

CHAPTER **19**

The First and Worst Month

January, 2010

January is a wicked step-mother of a month. Contradictory and contemptuous, January is sun, rain and snow, all in a half-hour's time. It's slushy toboggan runs and black ice on I-75. January is your passive-aggressive co-worker who smiles in your face then shoves daggers of ice in your back. It's not surprising, since the month is named after a two-faced Roman god.

It's 31 days of endurance that don't even fit on the standard calendar page. They have to swipe two other days and split them in half diagonally so January can have its cake and beat it too.

January is the flu. If May and June are presidential, January is Sarah Palin.

All any of us can hope for is that we're able to sneak through January without arousing suspicion. It can be meaner than a snake with a skin condition if provoked.

December got it right. It serves up Hanukkah, Christmas and New Year's, so we can have fun and forget the drudgery outside. February is shy, silent and elusive. It wants so badly to get out of the way and not be noticed that it shrinks back to 28 days and even gives us a vernal tease with Spring Training and that silly groundhog thing.

But January, snot-nosed and belligerent, just won't give up. "Hey, I'm still here," it cackles, then goes back into its frigid dank hole.

Remember back in the good ol' days before global warming and Perez or Paris Hilton? Back then, January would beat and rob you, then leave you to die in the snow. Snow? It used to be the one good thing that January could pretend to have invented. Nowadays we barely get enough to cover the pumpkins on foreclosed porches.

Down south somewhere, in Australia or Swaziland, January is probably a celebrated month. Perhaps that's its last and greatest irony. Some people welcome and revere the month because it's sunny and 70 and sublime. But if you spend any time in the Midwest, you'll learn to despise every cold, gray, wet, angry day of it. If not, well, you're not human ... or you're just visiting from New Zealand.

CHAPTER 20

EXCLUSIVE: Interview with The Yak

January, 2010
   (When your mascot's downsized, you know you've got problems. I caught up with The Yak at a mascot basketball game Saturday at the University of Detroit. His hair needed attention after living in a large steamer trunk for months, but it was nothing a quick brushing couldn't fix. His translator and I were laid off from the Detroit Free Press on the same day and it was good to see him after so many months. He agreed to an informal sit-down interview since neither of us were doing much at the time. No one knows his true identity and he asked me to respect that. Even in Layoff Land you can take the man out of The Yak, but you can't take The Yak out of the man.)

Rodney: So Mr. Yak, what have you been doing since that fateful day in June?
The Yak: Oh, freelance work here and there. I've been decorating some bars for the seasons; Halloween,

Christmas, I even did a great "*Marty*" Gras display at The Inn Place (*http://bit.ly/VN2Vbi*) in Royal Oak.

Rodney: "*Marty*" Gras, interesting choice of words. When did you know that things were going south at the paper; what tipped you off?

The Yak: That's easy, when The Yak section went online only. Everyone else took buyouts and I was the only one left in the department.

Rodney: I'd say that's a dead giveaway. Is it harder to forage for food and sustenance these days in this climate?

The Yak: The climate's great actually. The cold weather makes the suit more livable and I don't sweat as much. I remember one time, when we traveled to Orlando, a woman handed me a baby in a soiled diaper to hold. It was 95 degree heat and that smell just wafted into the outfit. *That* climate was tough.

Rodney: That's not what I meant by climate. Speaking of diapers, is it boxers or briefs?

**The Yak:** Depends.

Rodney: Depends (*http://www.depend.com/*), I get it. Funny. You've gone all over the world. What are some of your more memorable Yak trips?

The Yak: Well, the Olympics are on now, and we used to travel to those venues to preview them for the children; Japan, Australia, Italy, Utah. In Rome, some kid almost set me on fire until photographer Rashaun Rucker kicked his ass. I was attacked in New York City's Chinatown with firecrackers too, but mostly it was just a bunch of great times and fantastic travels.

Rodney: Ah, Ray Rucker. Glad he had your wing, err, your hoof. Hey, I've always wanted to know this. Which synonym for Yak makes you madder, "vomit" or "chatty?"

The Yak: Oh, "chatty" I suppose, but I don't really get mad at either one.

Rodney: I was just being silly. Along those same lines, and I know this is a sensitive subject, but I Googled Yak products and supposedly your cheese is high in Omega-3 acids, the good fat. Do you, uh, eat your own cheese?

The Yak: Just my toe cheese. We've all done it.

Rodney: As long as I'm on ridiculous topics, we both worked for the Detroit Daily Press. What do you think went wrong there?

The Yak: That place was a cluster fuck; I'm surprised it lasted five days.

Rodney: I hear you. So what will you write down on the 2010 Census when it comes to your mailbox?

The Yak: Unemployed, will work for food.

Rodney: I guess being The Yak, your employment opportunities are somewhat limited.

The Yak: I'm thinking about stripping on weekends. It's come to that.

Rodney: Now there's an image. Seriously, what are you looking to do next?

The Yak: I've applied for several jobs in graphics and

design. I'm looking to decorate more bars, do some business cards. There's work in Traverse City; I'd love to live there.

Rodney: I really appreciate you taking the time to Yak with me. Oops, you hate that. I also want to thank you for suggesting that I do the freelance work for this basketball game. Is there anything else you want to tell us?

The Yak: I went downtown to pick up the costume the other day and was invited to come into the newsroom. It just felt too weird, so I didn't. I do miss the people I used to work with at the Detroit Free Press, though. Tell them that.

With that, The Yak readied to run out to center court. The players left for halftime and Mayor Bing, a former basketball star himself, watched as the mass of mascots were introduced (*http://bit.ly/12Yjfi0*).

CHAPTER **21**

What I Think They Should Have Called the iPad

January, 2010

If you were like me, you couldn't wait until Steve Jobs came down from the mountain with his long-awaited tablet and issued our latest consumer commandments. What would the new tablet be called? I'd been channeling Nostradamus (*well, History Channeling him*), and came up with a list of possibilities before the actual announcement.

The iKea: You have to put it together yourself.

The iRonic: It's the opposite of whatever you're expecting.

The iStrain: It'll actually be smaller than the iPhone. Look for the *iStrain Nano* in time for summer.

The iHop: This fascinating device will be flatter than a pancake.

The iRaq: It'll cost you and your children's children billions of dollars.

The iWitness: Since every news organization is shrinking, just turn this machine on and it will gather all the news in its own WiFi hotspot.

The iMax: It's 100 feet tall and 300 feet wide when unfurled but actually folds down to the size of an iTunes gift card.

The iScream: A thrill ride/horror movie in one portable device.

The iOwa: It's flat, corny and boring.

The iMdb: It contains every movie ever made and interesting tidbits about Kevin Bacon.

The iRs: This nifty machine will actually hide all your income in the iTunes Store.

The iZod: It'll be dressy, yet remarkably casual.

The iUd: Uhhhh, nevermind.

CHAPTER **22**

Remaining Relevant

January, 2010
   One peril of having a birthday in your 40s is appearing old and stale. I don't wear those pointy hats anymore or yearn for pony rides. Comfy cargo pants and a few good books are on my wish list. Right now, my February birthday is still something I look forward to; my wife's, my eldest daughter's and my own are all in the same week, so it becomes a gala. But I can see the day in the not-so-distant future when I'll groan instead of smile as early February looms. Strangely, that's the same thing I face with blogging.
   Right now I'm groaning at my blog as the newest post withers and dries up. The iPad post is *so last Wednesday*, and even though it received a tremendous number of hits, now it's about as useful and relevant as Jon Gosselin or The Octomom. When you write a book, people understand that it freezes your thoughts at the moment of publication; they don't expect updates or tweets. Put

your thoughts online and, POW, if you don't have a pointy-hat-wearing-pony every couple of days, you too, risk irrelevance.

But what do you write about on the last day of January as a few melancholy snowflakes swirl around your neighbor's chimney, as seen from your study floor? How do you smack the occasional reader in the jaw with powerful prose that leaves a black and blue mark and makes them beg for one more hit? How do you interest even yourself?

Oh, I suppose you could write about the moment earlier today where you sat on the floor crying with your daughter about how she's growing up so fast and how, even though you're so proud of her accomplishments, sometimes, in the pit of your psyche, you miss the little girl she once was.

You could tell your blog about how even during these bleak times of only earning one-seventh of what you used to earn, you still seem happier than you were before. No, your blog wouldn't necessarily believe you, but maybe some of your readers would. If you believe it in your gut, they will too (*at least that's what you tell your magazine writing class*).

And Rodney, you might just want to openly opine about why you're hesitating to attend an upcoming photo conference because you lost two photo editing jobs in 2009. But there's a rawness there, a bit of an exposed nerve that hasn't scabbed or scarred up enough yet.

No, it's best if you remain quiet and not write half-formed thoughts just to have something different or new or fresh. Just keep that funny Steve Jobs post there atop your blog and enjoy the few stragglers that wander in, late to the party. Don't open the barn door too wide. All the ponies could escape.

CHAPTER 23

Stalked by a Balloonatic

February, 2010

A student in my class did the unthinkable. When we went around the room introducing ourselves, she was open and honest about something that really bothered her. She confessed to having a strange fear of balloons.

Big mistake.

That was all I needed to hear. I'm helping teach an online reporting class where we show the students how to use multimedia tools to tell their stories. As an example, I took my little Panasonic Lumix (*http://cnet.co/12Yjfi2*) point-n-shoot camera and created a wacky two-minute video.

I didn't think the fear of balloons was a real affliction until I wandered across globophobia (*http://bit.ly/12Yjfi5*) in my research. Some people just experience a vague uneasiness around them, others actually fear deflated ones. Apparently, Maury Povich did a whole show on this phobia. I had to overcome a vague

uneasiness about watching Maury in order to continue my research.

I ran into other quirky fears like arachibutyrophobia, which is—I'm not kidding—the fear of peanut butter sticking to the roof of your mouth. Podophobia, which, strangely, several of my students claim to have, is the fear of feet. But my favorite is the aptly named hippopotomonstrosesquippedaliophobia, the fear of long words.

It's no telling how many millions of children are scarred for life after being forced to sing Supercalifragilisticexpialidocious (*http://bit.ly/1bCQur3*) along with that mean Mary Poppins.

Normally, I'm a sensitive, caring, new-millennium man, but I couldn't stop laughing about my student's fear. When I showed this movie in class, they couldn't stop laughing either. My anonymous student loved it too and actually asked for a copy of this movie on DVD.

So, if you suffer from kainophobia, the fear of anything new, I suggest you click elsewhere. And if you're afflicted by geliophobia (*http://bit.ly/1bCQwPI*), the fear of laughter, cover your ears.

And eyes.

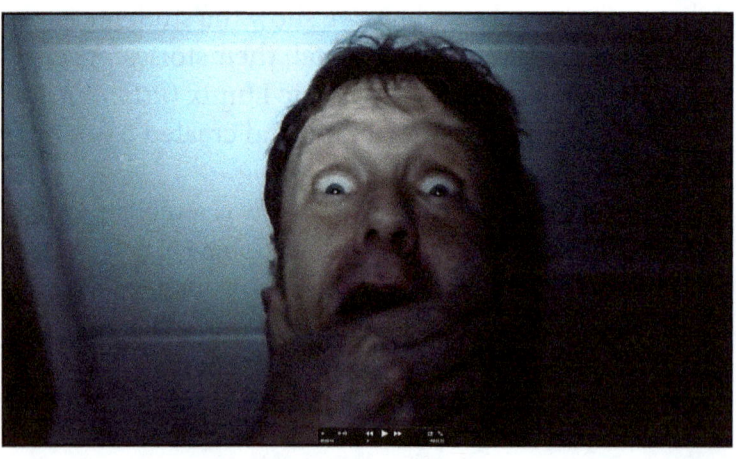

CHAPTER **24**

Home Wrecker

March, 2010

My work out here is coming to an end.

I flew to LA on a super-saver, last-minute, bags-extra flight in order to help my brother and sister-in-law renovate their new house, soak up some March sun and just do some overall latitude adjustment.

Alas, as a home handyman, my strengths lie in programing the DVR and making sure I close the refrigerator door. Oh, I can vacuum up a storm and make neat little piles of other people's stuff to be dealt with later, but let's just say my sister-in-law May's initial request that I do a bit of drywall patching when I woke up Sunday morning was met with a reasoned, "Umm…"

Thankfully, they were employing a real handyman who knew the difference between drywall and dry white wine. So it was on to my next task: laying their kitchen tile.

Umm...

Bag after 50-pound-bag of grout and tile cement lay stacked in their garage, along with newly purchased trowels, a couple pallets full of beautiful clay tiles, and one man's dream of becoming a Mason after reading Dan Brown's The Lost Symbol (*http://bit.ly/12Yjfi7*). The directions for the tile cement were easy enough, so after measuring three times and using an old cup we found lying around, (and calling my brother at work who had internet access and the ability to convert ounces to quarts), I got to mixing.

Fifty pounds of lifting and half an hour later I was ready to flop down my first square kitchen tile. Unfortunately, I had mistakenly mixed up the grout instead of the cement.

May and Areal, the Filipino handyman, exchanged polite looks and said a few words to each other in Tagalog (*http://bit.ly/12Yjfi8*). Note to self: look up the translation for "*dumbass.*"

Another 50 pounds and another half hour, and I was ready. The creamiest tile cement you ever saw flowed from my bucket of wonder, and we were ready to slap down that ceremonial first tile—with hidden coins for prosperity underneath—the hopes of at least getting something right riding on every move.

Apparently you don't want creamy tile cement on your floors.

Areal took the bucket back to the garage and hand-stirred another couple pounds of the powder into my concoction. He came back within moments, carrying actual tile cement. I glopped it down, said a few incantations to the holy Bob Villa and all went according to plan. That is, until the second tile went in a good three inches lower than the first. Okay, I'm exaggerating, but not by much. The first tile was like a platform, a mesa, a scenic overlook in a kitchen that wasn't planning to have an island.

Apparently you want your entire floor ... what's the word ... level.

By now, I was familiar with the Filipino word for "*incompetent*," although I have to say, May was nothing but gracious and amazingly sweet. I honestly don't know how she stomached having me in her brand new kitchen, mucking up all their first-time-homeowner plans.

Fully giving up any of his real plans for the day, Areal took the trowel, lifted the original tile, spread the cement properly and dropped it back into place, thus narrowly avoiding Ty Pennington and the Extreme Home Makeover team crashing through the kitchen wall.

They found a job I could do. The tiles were a few differing shades, between something that looked like yellow and red, to something that looked like red and yellow. They wanted a chaotic randomness to the arrangement on the floor.

Bingo!

For the next couple hours I busied myself with the artistic directorship of grabbing the tiles May was sealing in another room and painstakingly arranging them for Areal's final installation. I felt like the little boy in his mom's kitchen who's given the very important task of holding onto the egg so it doesn't roll away.

Yes, I was called upon to mix up another batch of cement and yes, I screwed that up too. As a general rule, you don't want a quarter of the mix still in powder form at the bottom of the bucket when you're through. And THAT'S a little free home improvement tip brought to you by the management team of Spiritual Wanderer International.

This is one of the reasons I don't do Habitat for Humanity builds. I'd be the guy serving sandwiches to the real workers and trying not to spill lemonade onto their freshly laid carpet. Everybody has a talent.

"If I had a hammer, I'd poke somebody's eye-eye out, I'd use the wrong end, and drop it in the grout."

My final task out here is to do some videotaping of my brother Dean's class at UCLA. I don't have to mix anything except maybe sound, and thank God, Allah, Buddha and Lugh (*http://abt.cm/12YjhX9*) there's no grout involved.

I think this pretty well puts to rest my notion of saving a bit of money by refinishing our hardwood floors while I'm laid off. I thought maybe Marci could strap sandpaper to the dogs' paws and make 'em run around like crazy while I'm stirring up the polyurethane in the garage.

What could possibly go wrong?

CHAPTER 25

The One Where I Drive My Mother to the Death Panel at the Local Walmart

March, 2010
(Now that the Obama health initiative has passed, I figured there was no time like the present to get my Mom an appointment with a Death Panel. Oh, don't worry, she's fine, fit-as-a-fiddle, and could walk rings around most middle-aged folks (and does when she circles the mall during her daily aerobic walks). But all good things must come to an end, so I picked her up and took her to Walmart.)

"Rodney, why is it again that we're going shopping?" she asked, as the warm March sunshine streamed through the passenger's window.

"Well, I suppose I should tell you the truth Ma, I don't really need your help picking out the best peanut butter."

"So your story about the choosiest mothers was all ... what?"

"As you've probably heard Mom, something called National Health Care is now the law of the land," I began explaining.

"Uh, honey, I'm not senile, remember those links I emailed you last week?"

"Sure, sure, they were sooo cute. I loved the little kitties playing with yarn."

"That wasn't me Rodney, I sent the New York Times piece dealing with misconceptions about the health care overhaul."

"Oh right, right. That was sooo cute. You actually believed this bill would be good for America, cover a whole bunch of people who never had coverage before, and save families money."

"Well, didn't you say, honey, that your family already has saved thousands of dollars in health care costs since Obama became president?"

"Yes, we did, but don't change the subject," I said as I found a spot in the crowded parking lot.

"Speaking of the subject at hand, what are we doing here?" she asked, as her long paces easily outdistanced my puny strides.

"Mom, you're in your 70s now; it's time to meet with the Death Panel."

Stopping a few yards in front of me, my dear old mother turned on a dime and gave me the stink eye.

"You're taking me to a Death Panel? Those things aren't real; they were fabricated by Republicans looking for any idiotic excuse to scare decent Americans."

"Oh, they're real alright, Mother dear," I say with a sneer, "and after today, you'll be on their list."

"I've never spanked you Rodney, ever. But right now I'm sorely tempted to … "

"Easy there Ma, I think your dementia may be kicking in."

"I'll dementia you. IF YOUR FATHER WERE ALIVE TODAY HE'D …"

"See Mom, not completing your sentences is a sure sign that you … "

"YOU KEEP CUTTING ME OFF!"

"Okay, okay," I reason, "let's just calm down and see what the nice people at Walmart have to say."

"Rodney, you've fallen into the propaganda trap. No one's killing anyone, except for that stupid Mike Cox, Michigan's attorney general, who's trying to say affordable health care for minorities and the underprivileged is unconstitutional."

"Come on Mom, no one's going to listen to that blowhard. He had a press conference a couple years ago saying he was unfaithful and had cheated on his wife."

"I remember, he made her stand right there next to him. What a jerk."

"That 'jerk' is running for governor."

"Good luck with that. Anyway, why are we really here?" she asks, as we head toward the optical kiosk.

In answer, I ring the buzzer and an overworked, underpaid woman slides the glass door open. I tell her we're here for the Death Panel and she sighs, checks her watch, gets on the loud speaker and calls for a quorum.

Apparently, corporate rules dictate that Walmart needs four people per panel and one can't convene until they're all in place. A greeter from the front is walking by and gets tagged to join the team. Someone wanders over from Children's Apparel and an obviously bored teen heading out for his smoke break can't veer quickly enough and gets sucked in.

"Okay, I assume you've all watched the 20 minute video in the break room," says the optical department receptionist.

Heads nod, except for the greeter's, who is on her cell phone.

chapter 25 • 75

"We have five minutes to decide how this woman should die. Any thoughts?"

My Mom chimes in, "Uh, yes. I have one. When Sarah Palin brought up Death Panels, it was named Lie Of The Year (*http://on.wsj.com/12Yjfi9*). Even conservatives think it's a whacked-out myth. What makes you think any of this is real?"

I notice my mother is starting to get the upper hand in this debate, so I resort to lies. "Mom, you sound like a Liberal. Don't you know Liberals hate America? (*http://bit.ly/12YjhXf*). Ann Coulter said that."

"Coulter also said it's a dream of hers to take away women's right to vote (*http://bit.ly/18VKY3U*)."

"Mom, if you can't take this seriously, we'll have to restrain you."

"Rodney honey, look around you, no one's left," she says, and sure enough, the only person remaining is the greeter, who's still on her cell and not paying attention.

"So, what you're saying is this whole Death Panel thing was another made-up excuse not to give health care to 36 million Americans?" I ask.

Knowingly, my mother nods. Realizing I had bought into a whole pack of lies, I hang my head, look around absently, shift my weight from one foot to the other and then apologize.

"Ma, I'm sorry. I didn't really want you dead anyway."

"I know sweetie. I know. But next time, let's stop believing all the Conservative lies."

"What about the weapons of mass destruction in Iraq?" I ask.

"Oh honey."

Can't get enough? Here I am reading the same thing you just read. (http://bit.ly/13XT1af)

CHAPTER **26**

Filet-O-Feet

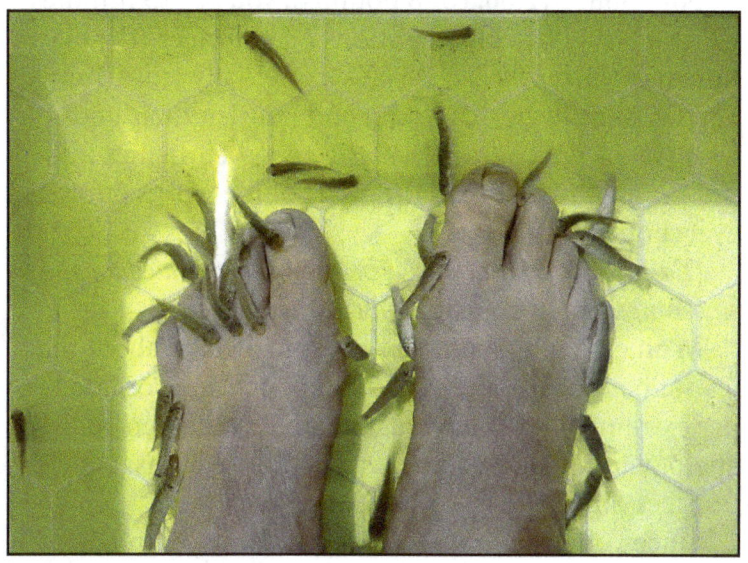

April, 2010

It's been several hours since the fish ate the dead skin off my feet, but I can still feel the tingling. When it comes to exfoliating, nothing beats a bucket full of minnows. (*http://bit.ly/12Yjfyr*)

I felt kind of bad for James, the guy standing there all alone in his flesh-eating-fish stall. He had a wonderful smile and a cheery good humor toward his job. As we continued to talk, I realized it was time to bare my feet and give the fish their breakfast. Yes, it was their first meal of the day.

(Editor's Note: this would be the normal place for me to say something like, "at first it seemed kind of fishy to me.")

As the story goes, the foot/flesh/fish guy was helping mind his friend's booth in Camden Town, a part of London. His friend had first seen these fish in Thailand, where they are apparently very popular. He introduced the concept to the western world and it's been a pretty lucrative business so far.

For about $12.00, (or 8 pounds), you get 15 minutes worth of tingly, tickly sensations on your feet. The Garra Rufa fish (*http://bit.ly/12YjhXk*), originally from Turkey, thrives off the dead skin, and nourish their body with your flakey outer layer. They get their bellies full, you get an all-day buzz. The circle of life works out for everybody.

(Editor's Note: this would be the normal place for me to say something like, "nothing beats filet of sole.")

In an earlier chapter, you can find a video about the fear of balloons—because a student of mine confided her extreme phobia towards them. This is a personal apology to my other students who told the class they fear feet (*http://bit.ly/18VKY3W*).

Since you can always believe whatever you read on the Internet, I'm told the procedure is completely safe, diseases aren't transmitted from person-to-fish-to-person, and spas all over the world are now beginning to offer the treatment for a lot more than 12 bucks.

Do I recommend the experience? Sure. Did I do it because it was odd and thought it would be fun to write about? Definitely. Regardless of the motivation or outcome, my dead skin sleeps with the fishes.

(Editor's Note: I didn't actually come up with that last joke. Our teen traveling companion Gaia thought it up.)

CHAPTER 27

Get Your Kicks on Route 666

April, 2010

(My editors at Read The Spirit (http://bit.ly/R022xO) were planning on skipping their 666th magazine article. They number each of their articles for easy reference but I convinced them not to jump from 665 to 667. Here's what I wrote. Maybe they should've skipped it after all.)

Apart from Rep. Michelle Bachmann, I don't believe evil really exists as a force in the cosmos. This has gotten me in trouble time and again, from basically evil people. Not believing they exist tends to make them a bit ornery.

A famous personal conversation that I've retold many times happened between me and a former boss. She brought up the subject saying, "You know Rodney, the difference between us is—you believe people are basically good and I know they're bad."

It was in reference to giving our staff the benefit of the doubt, and she was unwilling to believe someone had made an honest mistake. It perfectly highlighted the chasm existing between those of us who see the glass half full and those who think someone drank the other half while our heads were turned.

Do I believe in God? Yes. Can I define God? Heavens no. Do I believe in the devil? Sorry Charlie. Do I think people do really bad things? Look no further than the people who invented Jersey Shore (*http://on.mtv.com/12Yjfyx*) for your answer.

But imagining evil as a force, a cognizant power that floats or creeps around the planet looking for a weak human to do its bidding is just unfathomable to me. And yet, I believe in a force for good that does just that. Weird, eh?

I posed the question to my family after driving home from Five Guys Burgers and Fries (*http://bit.ly/12YjidC*), our newest unhealthy-yet-totally-yummy obsession. Did any of them believe evil existed in the world? Now granted, this was a small sample of the entire human population, but it's the most important sampling to me. None of my ladies felt in their hearts that a Satan or a devil or a Bernie Madoff stalks the planet looking for victims to do his bidding.

Yet each of us agreed there is some kind of co-voyager with us, both 21st century and ancient, who nudges us via coincidence or conscience along the right path. I happen to believe He/She/It helped me write that last sentence. But that's just me. I wouldn't want to impose my beliefs on anyone else. Although if you've read this far, I'm kind of doing just that.

What about Hitler, Pol Pot or those responsible for the Rwandan genocide? Surely, they were evil or proof that evil exists. Ah, that's where our philosophy hits an icy patch. I don't expect you to come away from this completely buying into my world view. Hitler and crew did some very bad things. Horrifically so, obviously. There's no denying—unless you're the Iranian president—that what they did were some of the worst atrocities ever committed on this planet.

I believe, however, that they were just individuals or massive groups of individuals doing terrible things. Did they have the capacity to love? Probably. Were they mentally ill? Probably. Was there a nefarious force that used their weaknesses to do its diabolic work? Probably not. It's like my mother used to say to me when I was little, "No Rodney, I don't hate you; I hate what you did, but I don't hate you."

Wait, it's not really like that at all. But you get the point.

Maybe you don't.

Is there hate in this world? Duh. If you don't believe in hate I'm coming over to kick your butt. *(Note to the world, I couldn't kick a rump roast's butt).*

The worst of the worst members of our planetary history were more than likely suffering from mental illnesses that brought about delusions or impossibly terrible decisions. If they weren't sick, they chose their actions out of badly misguided beliefs or thought constructs that none of their associates were able to stop. Were there actual, tangible demons sitting there whispering in these despot's ears? Hell no!

The thing that shocks me awake at 4:00 a.m. though, the thing that whispers into my own soul when I'm asleep is …

What if I'm wrong?

CHAPTER **28**

In or Out

April, 2010

"Dear Mr. Curtis, We received a high number of applications from extremely well-qualified candidates. The pool was so outstanding that we regret that we have only one position available. We have now filled the position. Unfortunately, our search ended this year without making a hire."

I wasn't asking for much, just a job teaching journalism. But my rejection letter, received from an anonymous accredited university, left me laughing. Not getting picked to play on their team is one thing. I understand

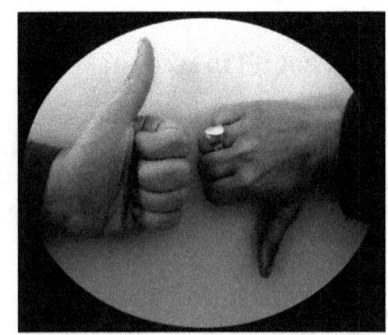

that I may not have all the requisite tools: hitting, fielding, slugging percentage *and* clubhouse demeanor. But what I do have is a pretty good understanding of how to string a group of sentences together. Apparently that's not a prerequisite for this particular college, (*oh slam-snap*).

When I shared their mishmash of a letter on Facebook, I had a couple dozen responses. To paraphrase my buddy Neal Rubin, **if they wrote one more sentence you'd be officially hired.**

I understand that sometimes you run into cut and paste failures, as others on Facebook pointed out. And I'm sure if I ever met the individual who sent it, they'd be horrified at their mistake. Mostly though, it left me longing for the day in the not-so-distant future when all the Baby Boomers start retiring and the jobs will flow like milk and honey. Some estimates even put the job glut at the five million mark (*http://bit.ly/12YjidE*).

Until that day arrives, I'll keep sending out job applications. Although they most likely won't be like the ones I sent back in the 80s, which contained free Ginsu knives, as seen on TV, (*"Even if you return the portfolio, keep the Ginsu as a free gift just for examining my work."*)

Yes, I really did that. No, it never got me a job.

Too bad the Shake Weight (*http://bit.ly/1bCQwPQ*) hadn't been invented yet.

chapter 28 • 83

CHAPTER **29**

Grow With the Flow

May, 2010

Since I got laid off 11 months ago, I've made it my goal to go with the flow. Yes, I sound like a new age hippie from ages gone by, but there's been this undeniable force leading me along some as-of-yet unknown path. Maybe it's God, or The Universal Flow, or my dead Dad or my conscience. Whatever it is, I've felt the subtle pressure, like a horse or mule must feel when being driven by an experienced master. Yes, I just called myself God's jackass.

It's been there consistently as minor and major decisions have arisen, and since I have more time in my life these days, I've made it a point to stop, center myself, and consult the flow. The crazy thing is, it's not too difficult to listen to. I know straight away what the answer is in most cases, even if I don't want to hear it. When I was curled up in a ball on my living room floor a few Sunday nights ago, I asked the flow what to do. Even though it answered, "What do you think, idiot? Get to the emergency room," I still waited another half hour. My now discarded gall bladder may have wanted me to wait longer, but the rest of my body thanked me after the operation.

There have been a few times when I purposely asked the flow what to do and blatantly disregarded the answer, since I knew better.

The most memorable time was when a new job opened up that I had been dreading, but decided to take, since we could've used the money. It, of course, was the ill-fated Detroit Daily Press, which lasted all of five days.

Every fabric of my being, along with other fabrics, like rayon and polyester, told me this wasn't the job for me. Still, I went for it, got chewed up for several weeks during the planning and implementation, then spit out when the damn thing closed after less than a week of actual newspapers. They still owe me money, but it was a great learning tool. Trust your instincts.

I wrote a blog entry that I never posted back in March. I was saving it for some reason. Being a little hesitant about it, March became April and April segued into May. After numerous reworkings and rewordings I finally got the guts to let it go live. I had heard that the chief of my former company—the one that laid me off—made millions and millions of dollars last year in bonuses and salary. So, I challenged him to a boxing match. I made up a cool old-fashioned boxing promoter's poster and had funny jabs left and right. I even called it Throwdown In Motown.

It was classic "Rodney," if you'll allow me to make those dopey air quotes around my name. I was nervous about this big time; I can't say why, I just felt weird about it. This past Sunday I hit the PUBLISH button, informed the wise folks in the home office, and even sent a note to a blogger who covers the company. Half an hour later I received an email back from that blogger saying I should tread gingerly; the man in question had an operation last year and—not many people know this—he's been in a wheelchair ever since. I may be a lot of things, but insensitive I'm not. There's no way I'd sucker punch an invalid, even in written form. I yanked the posting immediately.

So there again, something deep within me was screaming and I just put in the earplugs and bumbled forth. I'm beginning to see, as the wisdom from my accumulated years seeps in, that stuff works out.

Even if it doesn't exactly follow a perfect path, stuff works out. See the epilogue for an opposing point of view.

CHAPTER 30

Once Bitten, Twice Wry

May, 2010

I feel like I should be doing something constructive. It seems as though I have this embarrassing wealth of time on my hands and I'm squandering it surfing the web, caring a little too much about the Detroit Tigers pitching and having conversations with people about, well, squandering all this time on my hands.

I've discussed this with my wife, my kids, college buddies and friends from past lives. Mostly journalism past lives, not the Shirley MacLaine version. The consensus appears to be that excess time on your side isn't really something to worry about. Come back to us when you have real problems. Actually, most everyone has been supportive.

It's not like I haven't been looking for work. I've run the gamut from serious to silly. Sure, maybe my application for a teaching position with a concentration in photography may appear rational on the surface, but if you happened to notice that I was applying to be a headmaster in an all-girls' school in East London, you

probably realized I was being a bit too unrealistic. I'll leave it up to you to determine if my Ghost Ranch (*http://bit.ly/12YjfOU*) application was sane, or the workings of someone who is steadily losing touch with reality.

I'm far more involved in my daughter's lives these days and they still seem to think that's a good thing. My oldest, Skye, told me this morning, "You're just taking time out of the rat race until you can figure out what you're racing for."

As I sneak up on my layoff anniversary, I can honestly say I'm much closer with my wife and far more in tune with everything familial. But there's that gnawing bit of societal pressure which tells me writing blogs and creating eBooks and caring too much about my lawn are not acceptable vocations. I've written about things I've tried over the past year that haven't come to fruition or produced much money. I'm still trying to figure out whether I'm gun-shy now because of them. Does the resounding silence from the job applications dim my spirits? Did my dismissal from the Free Press put a hitch in my giddyup? Did my job that never even really started at the Detroit Daily Press sour me on the future of print journalism? Or does my unknown future as an educator leave me nervous? Actually, I think all those things are in play. It's sometimes tough to get excited about another position, or get your hopes up about something new when in the back of your head you still haven't heard bupkus from the previous thing you invested your energy in. It's hard not to be cynical.

Once bitten, twice wry.

It's something you don't hear a lot about: the guilt over not doing a damn thing. I try to justify it by pretending what I do during the day actually matters. And yes, according to my friends, stuff I write and invest my time in *does actually matter*. When my wife's off bringing home the bacon, it just feels weird to point to a freshly mown lawn and say, "Look how much work I did today, honey."

But it would feel equally weird to tell my daughters I couldn't take them to this activity or that function because I had to go steam cappuccinos at my barista job that didn't pay me any more than my unemployment benefits already are. I actually owe it to them to keep creating, to keep following my dream of getting paid to write. If I give up now, what would I be telling them? "Uh ladies, remember Daddy's directive to follow your passions? You should probably only do that after your 2 - 10 shift at Qdoba (*http://www.qdoba.com/*).

(This is a private note between me and Anthony Miller & Robert Hauser, Qdoba's founders: I just gave you free publicity. What say you slide me a free Poblano Pesto Burrito?)

I'm going to continue pretending that what I'm doing now is valuable and enriching and necessary. Yes, of course, I'm still on the hunt for gainful employment. And just so you know, I'm happy to mow your lawn if you live in Metro Detroit. But I have to wrap this piece up pretty quickly. The Tigers are about to play and I think Verlander's taking the mound.

CHAPTER **31**

Re-enlisting in the Unemployment Army

June, 2010

It's been a year since my layoff and I just now used up the last of my six-month supply of unemployment benefits. I'm good at rationing, I guess.

When you take my three months of severance pay and mix in a pinch of dough from teaching, yeah, you can spread out the benefits to last a year. I have a feeling though, that my six month extension will be used up in about six months, or less, if that's possible. That makes me nervous. I think it makes my wife nervous too. But maybe it's because we sit back-to-back at our respective computers and have been doing so for most of the past year. I can tell when we're ticked off at each other; the dogs have to form a canine barrier between us. Soon, one of us will break the silence by either farting, or saying something disparaging about Republicans. When you don't feel like being snippy, detente is just a moment or two away.

Oh, oh, the rain just started to fall like crazy. "Do you hear that?" I ask. "The rain again," she responds. "No, Bernie licking himself," I say. And the tension washes away with a sigh.

So, back to these unemployment benefits. In the handy handout they gave me, it says I can receive extended pay only until the Michigan unemployment rate dips back below 6.5%. I figure that gives me cash until I "retire." This economic depression in the Great Lake State isn't going away any time soon.

I asked the helpful guy at the unemployment office if he's run into anything crazy and his response was immediate:

"I can't believe the politicians think people are happy to stay on extended benefits. When someone can't pay their car, home or other bills, they definitely aren't eating out or doing other things like that. It affects all of us, everywhere." I appreciated his answer. I felt better about being a strain on society. "Can I use your name?" I asked, "Or would you prefer to remain anonymous?" "Mmmm, better leave my name out of it."

He didn't want to end up right where I was sitting.

Now I have six more months of unemployment pay heading my way. I remember a time when writing something like that would've choked me up and made my fingers feel like peanut butter on the keyboard. But now, as I look for steady work in the **Arts, Design, Entertainment, Sports and Media** field, (as I'm categorized on the Michigan.gov website), I can hold my head high.

I wish, though, that they had more interesting pull-down menus. I would've given anything to click **Carnie/Roustabout**. Or **Dog Whisperer**.

CHAPTER **32**

(And now, a few extras as our free gift to you, our valued consumer.)

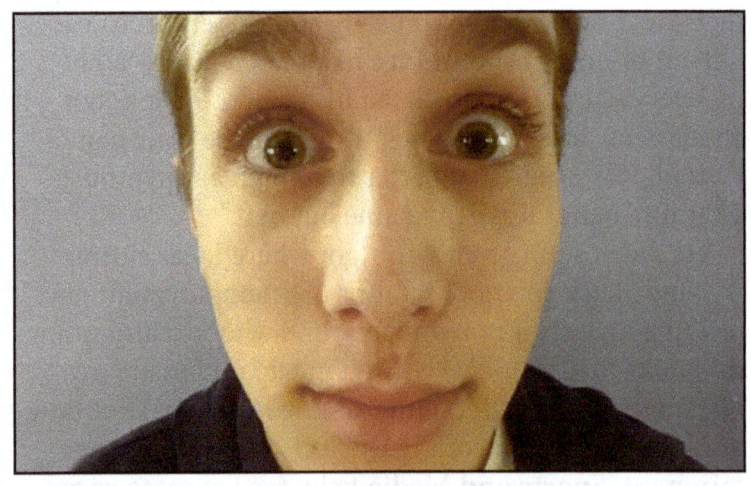

We're glad our friend Tony finally found his porpoise. (*http://bit.ly/12YjfOV*)

CHAPTER 33

Dog Duty

(NO STORY I'VE ever written has gotten more attention than this silly piece about my dog who poops the craziest things out his butt.)

Scooping poop in the backyard I noticed, quite clearly, a barcode sticking out from one of Bernie's turds. Being on doggie duty, I couldn't help but be amazed at how far-reaching the packaging phenomenon has spread. When crap comes out of your dog's butt already assigned a specific code, we've either taken a great leap forward in biotechnology, or Bernie has just gotten into something he shouldn't have. I almost wanted to wrap it in a Ziploc bag and take it to one of those free-standing store scanners and see what rang up.

"Clean up on aisle five!"

But that's not the most insane thing I've ever trowelled into an old shopping bag. A few Christmases ago my daughter Skye's advent calendar was plundered, and she immediately blamed her younger sister, Taylor. It wasn't until a few days later when, again on doggie duty, I noticed a trail of carnage of biblical proportions. There, sticking out of various backyard scat was, in no particular order, The Star of David, a present, a camel, an angel, two of the three wise men, and the Hamburglar. Speaking from my somewhat fuzzy recollection of the New Testament, I can account for most all of the aforementioned characters, except the Hamburglar.

"We've brought gold, frankincense, and myrrh, would you like fries with that?"

The weird part is, I salvaged the players from their turd tableau and brought them inside to our laundry tub and began the process of resurrection. I used a lot of water, far too much bleach and even some Febreze. They dried out over the ensuing days and I put them through the process again, with my wife's encouragement. And there they sat, on the rim of the sink for days, weeks, even months.

Along about April, when spring had finally spread across Michigan, I had a heart-to-heart with my wife and we decided there was no stinkin' way these figurines were ever going to be revered like they once were. So we did what we should have done back in December and tossed them in the trash. I don't think Skye noticed, or cared.

It reminded me of our earlier dog, Alex the Magician. He had extreme separation anxiety. Marci and I couldn't leave the house without him getting nervous that we'd never return. He'd start trashing the place like a 70s rock star on acid. We would go to the corner store for five minutes and upon our return, the kitchen was in tatters; drapes pulled down, plates broken on the floor, the water running somehow and a knife set half-chewed with a little blood splattered on the linoleum.

He once ate half a bottle of aspirin that was, we thought, hidden on top of the microwave. He didn't even leave a suicide note. Luckily, he was just down and depressed for 18 hours then back to his abnormal self. It was a day or so after yet another one of his wild kitchen incidents that I took him out for a stroll. He seemed normal at first, but as the walk progressed, he started doing that hilarious little butt drag that cracks me up every time I see a dog do it. He got in a sitting position and with his hind legs lifted off the ground, pulling his pooper along the grass with his front legs. People say they're trying to get rid of worms. Personally, I think it's a great way for worms to get *in* his butt. Anyway, he was doing this every ten or twenty steps, when I noticed something odd and amazing.

Little by little, something started snaking out of his rectum. By the third scoot, there was an unmistakable inch-and-a-half piece of blue and white fabric hanging from his anus. I had no idea what to do, so I turned back for home. As we made our way past subdivision homes gleaming in the afternoon sun, I realized that they had no idea about the miracle that was taking place right on their front lawns.

As we got closer and closer, the fabric got longer and longer and I realized, with shock and awe, that my dog was pulling a dishrag out of his behind. By the time we took another several steps the magician had produced a full foot-long blue and white, and yes, slightly brown, scarf. Nothing up his sleeves either! Doggy Copperfield!

It appeared that, for the moment, he was done and happy. His gait was back to normal and he seemed, for lack of a better description, to almost have a smile on his face. Yet, the blue Handi Wipe still dangled from his butt as we made our way home. And here, here I did something that defined me and my mission to make the world a better place.

I knew that the rag was stuck and couldn't just stay there. But I knew equally well that I had no desire to pull it out with my hands. So I found a stick, told him to heel, and I twirled the twig around the dangling doo-rag and pulled. The first tug produced nothing. The second brought out not only the remnants of the Handi Wipe, but a little, guttural, satisfied yelp from my dog. I half expected him to turn and bite me, but the passing left nothing more than a vague memory on his doggie conscience.

Leaving the rag by the side of the road, we headed home. Him with his intestines squeaky clean and me with an indelible mark on my psyche.

I've shared this story with my family and some college buddies. They say I need an ending, a conclusion to pull it all together. This April—after a long—gray winter, I was back out on the lawn scooping up Bernie's backyard bowel movements. And there, staring out at me, was Abraham.

Lest you think, dear reader, that Bernie had sent both New and Old Testament through his digestive tract, I must inform you that the Abraham I speak of was on the face of a formerly crisp, clean five dollar bill that went missing from our kitchen counter months earlier. In the same scat was half of a George Washington in the shape of a cylinder. The five fifty feces.

So yes, I've taken up money laundering. Hopefully the IRS won't mind. In the sink that formerly washed the Wise Men, there now sits another project awaiting my attention. Whereas we eventually tossed the advent figures, throwing money away is another story entirely. Although I can't think of a plan for passing off the fiver right now. Maybe the U.S. Mint has a special archive for curious currency. My wife says we can't get rid of Bernie, no matter how much of a pain he is. He makes for great stories. He's generally cuddly and loveable.

And he's got money coming out the wazoo.

Here's Alex eating something far more appropriate. (*http://bit.ly/12YjidR*)

Epilogue

I'M TOLD AN epilogue is used at the end of a piece of literature to bring a sense of closure. By that definition, this little tag-ending is hopelessly misnamed. First, this hardly qualifies as literature and second, I'm about to bring the exact opposite of closure—aperture, maybe?

Maybe it was because I wrote that dopey piece about not being afraid of 666. Perhaps it's just because I had extra time on my hands. Regardless, many of you know what happened almost immediately after I wrote the last chapter in this book, Once Bitten, Twice Wry.

I caught cancer.

Look for my book, A "Cute" Leukemia. (*http://bit.ly/1bCQwPT*)

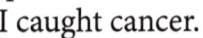

SPOILER ALERT: I lived.
Thanks for reading!
Rodney Curtis.

Colophon

READ THE SPIRIT Books produces its titles using innovative digital systems that serve the emerging wave of readers who want their books delivered in a wide range of formats—from traditional print to digital readers in many shapes and sizes. This book was produced using this entirely digital process that separates the core content of the book from details of final presentation, a process that increases the flexibility and accessibility of the book's text and images. At the same time, our system ensures a well-designed, easy-to-read experience on all reading platforms, built into the digital data file itself.

David Crumm Media has built a unique production workflow employing a number of XML (Extensible Markup Language) technologies. This workflow allows us to create a single digital "book" data file that can be delivered quickly in all formats from traditionally bound print-on-paper to nearly any digital reader you care to choose, including Amazon Kindle®, Apple iBook®, Barnes and Noble Nook® and other devices that support the ePub and PDF digital book formats.

And due to the efficient "print-on-demand" process we use for printed books, we invite you to visit us online to learn more about opportunities to order quantities of this book with the possibility of personalizing a "group read" for your organization by putting your organization's logo and name on the cover of the copies you order. You can even add your own introductory pages to this book.

During production, we use Adobe InDesign®, <Oxygen/>® XML Editor and Microsoft Word® along with custom tools built in-house.

The print edition is set in Minion Pro and Avenir Next.

Cover art and Design by Rick Nease: www.RickNeaseArt.com.

Copy editing by Dmitri Barvinok and Celeste Dykas.

XML styling, digital encoding and print layout by Dmitri Barvinok.

If you enjoyed this book, you may also enjoy

"He's a little bit of Dave Barry, David Sedaris and that fun quirky guy you met on an airplane once all rolled into one." —*from a review on Amazon.com*

http://www.SpiritualWanderer.com

ISBN: 978-1-934879-07-8

If you enjoyed this book, you may also enjoy

The shocking L-words struck like hammers: "Laid off," then, "Leukemia." Like millions of Americans, Rodney Curtis feared for his life and his family. Join Rodney on his quest to recover both his humor and his health.

http://A-Cute-Leukemia.com

ISBN: 978-1-934879-81-8

If you enjoyed this book, you may also enjoy

Suzy Farbman has entertained millions of readers throughout her career as a writer. You're in the hands of a wise, often funny and startlingly honest friend in the pages of her books.

http://www.GodsignsBook.com
ISBN: 978-1-934879-58-0

If you enjoyed this book, you may also enjoy

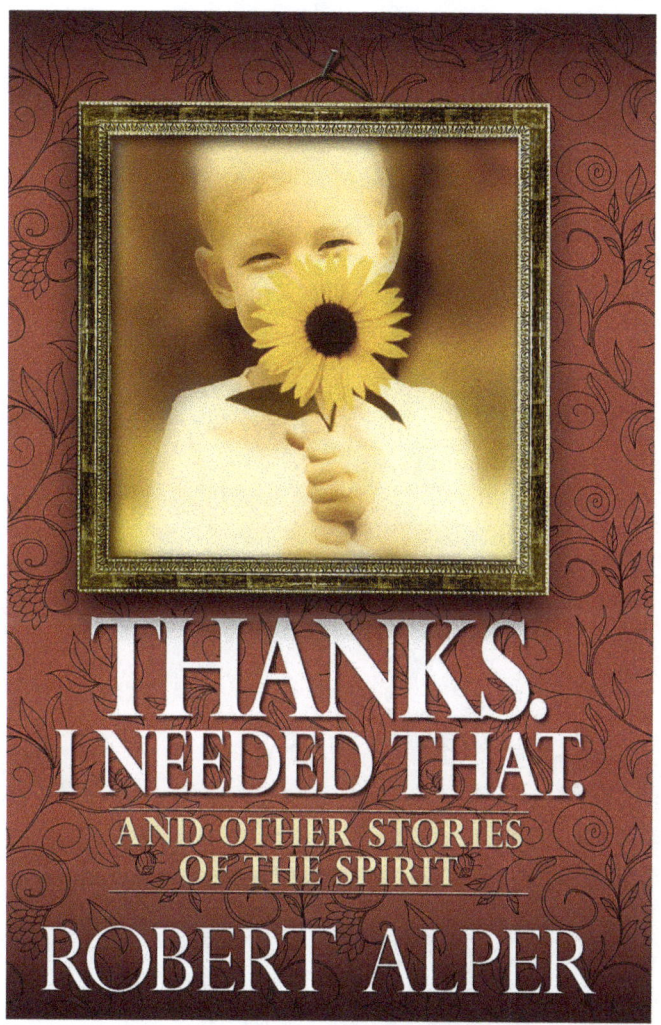

There's no storyteller like Rabbi Bob Alper, the world's only full-time stand-up comic and practicing rabbi. His true stories are heard daily on the Sirius/XM clean comedy channel.

http://INeededThat.info

ISBN: 978-1-934879-86-3

www.ingramcontent.com/pod-product-compliance
Lightning Source LLC
Chambersburg PA
CBHW062117080426
42734CB00012B/2893